My First Catechism

The Small Catechism
of
Dr. Martin Luther
illustrated with pictures
and narratives
from God's Word

CONCORDIA PUBLISHING HOUSE • SAINT LOUIS

Second Edition
Copyright © 2004, 2005 Concordia Publishing House
3558 S. Jefferson Ave., St. Louis, MO 63118-3968
1-800-325-3040 • www.cph.org

Prepared and edited by Rodney L. Rathmann; Erik Rottmann, consultant

Scripture quotations marked NIV are from the Holy Bible, New International Version®. NIV®
Copyright © 1973, 1978, 1984 by Biblica, Inc. Used by permission of Zondervan. All right
reserved.

Catechism quotations are from *Luther's Small Catechism with Explanation*, copyright © 1986, 199
Concordia Publishing House.

Manufactured in Shenzhen, China 022100/409279

4   5   6   7   8   9   10   20   19   18   17   16   15   1

Contents

Martin Luther delighted in teaching people, young and old alike, the truths about Christian life and salvation as found in God's holy Word. To assist families in learning and reviewing Christian doctrine, Luther wrote the Small Catechism in 1529.

Presented to

_____

By

_____

On

_____

The Ten Commandments

As the head of the family
should teach them in a simple way
to his household

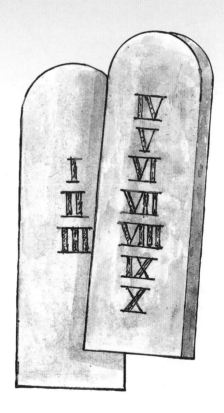

God gave the Ten Commandments to Moses and His people long ago on Mount Sinai.

Long ago God rescued His people from slavery in Egypt. He brought them from Egypt to a mountain called Sinai. With lightning and thunder and smoke and fire, God descended onto the mountain. God called Moses to come up to the mountain (Exodus 19:17–20). Here God wrote Ten Commandments on two flat pieces of stone. The commandments tell us how we are to live (Exodus 20:1–17). God gave us the commandments because He loves us. God sent Jesus to earn forgiveness for the times we break the commandments.

The First Commandment
You shall have no other gods.

Once a wicked king commanded all the people to bow down and worship a statue. The people did as the king commanded, except for three men who believed in God. When they refused to worship the statue, the king ordered them to be thrown into a hot furnace and burned. But God was with the men. He sent an angel to protect them in the furnace. The men who trusted in God were not burned. "Come out of the furnace!" called the king. "There is no god like your God. He saves His people!" (Daniel 3)

What does this mean? We should fear, love, and trust in God above all things.

Long ago God told a man named Abraham to take his son Isaac to a mountaintop. God told Abraham to sacrifice Isaac on an altar. Abraham and Isaac were willing to obey. But God was only testing their faith. Instead of Isaac, God provided a ram for the sacrifice (Genesis 22:1–19). Isaac reminds us of Jesus, the Lamb of God who willingly gave His life to save all people from their sins.

The Second Commandment

You shall not misuse the name of the Lord your God.

Once a giant named Goliath came onto the battlefield. He spoke against God and His people, challenging someone to fight him. David, a shepherd boy who trusted in God, heard the giant. When David came out onto the field to fight, Goliath cursed him. David said, "You come against me with sword and spear but I come against you in the name of the LORD Almighty." David swung his slingshot and released a stone. The stone hit Goliath in the forehead, knocking him dead. (1 Samuel 17:1–50; quote: NIV)

What does this mean? We should fear and love God so that we do not curse, swear, use satanic arts, lie, or deceive by His name, but call upon it in every trouble, pray, praise, and give thanks.

Daniel loved God. He prayed to God three times a day. When some evil men tricked the king into passing a law that no one should pray to God, Daniel kept on praying. The evil men had Daniel arrested because of his prayers. Daniel was thrown into a den of lions. But God sent an angel to keep the lions from harming Daniel. When the king saw that Daniel was unharmed, he took Daniel away from the lions. The king was very happy. "The God of Daniel is the living God," said the king. "He is the God who saves His people!" (Daniel 6)

The Third Commandment
Remember the Sabbath day by keeping it holy.

When Jesus was 12 years, He went with Mary and Joseph to Jerusalem to celebrate the Passover. On their return trip, Mary and Joseph couldn't find Jesus anywhere. They searched for Jesus among their family and friends. Then they hurried back to Jerusalem. After three days, they found Him with the teachers in the temple, listening to them and asking them questions. "Didn't you know I had to be in My Father's house?" Jesus asked. (Luke 2:41–50; quote: NIV)

What does this mean? We should fear and love God so that we do not despise preaching and His Word, but hold it sacred and gladly hear and learn it.

Once Jesus came to visit two sisters, Martha and Mary. Mary sat listening to Jesus' words. But Martha was busy working to make Jesus' stay pleasant and enjoyable. "Lord, tell Mary to come and help me," Martha suggested. But Jesus replied, "Martha, you are worried about many things, but only one thing is important. Mary has chosen that one thing. She is listening to God's Word." (Luke 10:38–42)

The Fourth Commandment
Honor your father and your mother.

God sent His Son to earth to be born a tiny baby. As He grew up, Jesus was obedient to Joseph and to His mother, Mary. As He got bigger, He became more and more helpful to His parents. People liked Jesus because He was kind and good (Luke 2:51–52). Jesus was holy. He obeyed His Father in heaven. Jesus lived a perfect life for us. Because Jesus came to save us, we are forgiven for the times we disobey our parents or do other bad things.

What does this mean? We should fear and love God so that we do not despise or anger our parents and other authorities, but honor them, serve and obey them, love and cherish them.

King David had a handsome son named Absalom. As people came to see the king, Absalom would say to them, "If I were king, I would see to it that you would get justice." David knew God's love and forgiveness and wanted to show love and forgiveness to Absalom. But Absalom led an army against his father, King David. While riding his mule to escape from David's soldiers, Absalom's head got caught in a tree, and the commander of David's army killed him. David was sad for Absalom. He said, "Oh, Absalom, my son! I wish I would have died instead of you!" (2 Samuel 15–18)

The Fifth Commandment
You shall not murder.

After Adam and Eve left the Garden of Eden, God gave them two sons, Cain and Abel. Cain grew up to become a farmer. Abel became a shepherd. Both Cain and Abel brought gifts to God. These gifts were burned on God's altar. Abel gave God the best he had. Cain did not. God was pleased with Abel's offering and not with Cain's. Cain became jealous of Abel and killed him. God gave Adam and Eve another son named Seth (Genesis 4). From Seth's family came the Savior, who died to take away all sins.

What does this mean? We should fear and love God so that we do not hurt or harm our neighbor in his body, but help and support him in every physical need.

Jesus once told this story: "A certain man was walking from Jerusalem to Jericho. On the way, some thieves robbed and wounded him and left him half dead. Later, a Samaritan came and helped the man. (Samaritans and Jews were enemies.) The Samaritan bandaged the man's wounds and took him to a place where he could receive care" (Luke 10:30–37). The Samaritan reminds us of Jesus. He came to help and save all people, including enemies and those who don't know Him.

The Sixth Commandment
You shall not commit adultery.

Once the teachers brought to Jesus a woman caught in adultery, meaning she had sinned with a man to whom she was not married. The teachers asked Jesus whether the woman should be stoned to death for her sin. Jesus bent down and wrote on the ground with His finger. "If any of you is without sin," Jesus said, "let him throw the first stone." One by one the people left until only the woman remained. Jesus forgave the woman. "Leave your life of sin," He told her. (John 8:1–11)

What does this mean? We should fear and love God so that we lead a sexually pure and decent life in what we say and do, and husband and wife love and honor each other.

Jesus wants people to be happy in marriage. Once Jesus attended a wedding in Cana. His mother and His disciples were also there. When the wine ran out, Mary asked Jesus to help. Jesus told the servants to fill six large jars with water. Jesus showed that He was Almighty God. He changed the water into wine! (John 2:1–11). God's Word tells us that Jesus' love for those who believe in Him is like the love of a husband who is willing to give his life for his wife. (Ephesians 5:22–25)

The Seventh Commandment
You shall not steal.

Shortly after God brought His people into the Promised Land, He gave them victory over the city of Jericho. God told the people not to take for themselves any of the things they found in the city. But Achan disobeyed. When he saw a beautiful robe, silver, and gold, he took these things for himself and hid them. But nothing can be hidden from God. Achan's sin was soon discovered (Joshua 7). Jesus calls us to repentance and offers forgiveness for all sins, including the sin of stealing.

What does this mean? We should fear and love God so that we do not take our neighbor's money or possessions, or get them in any dishonest way, but help him to improve and protect his possessions and income.

Zacchaeus was a chief tax collector and very rich. Because he was short, he climbed up into a sycamore-fig tree to see Jesus walking by. Jesus walked up to the tree. He said, "Come down, Zacchaeus. I want to stay at your house today." Zacchaeus came to believe in Jesus as his Savior. Jesus changed Zacchaeus's heart. Zacchaeus promised to give half of his possessions to the poor. If he had cheated anyone, he returned four times the amount. "I have come to seek and save the lost," Jesus said. (Luke 19:1–10)

The Eighth Commandment

You shall not give false testimony against your neighbor.

When Jesus' enemies arrested Him, they took Jesus to stand trial before the chief priest. The whole court was looking for false evidence against Jesus so they could put Him to death. Though many false witnesses came forward, none agreed with any other. Finally, the Chief Priest asked Jesus directly, "Tell us if You are the Christ, the Son of God." Jesus answered, "Yes." Jesus spoke the truth. But His reply made the Chief Priest so angry he tore his clothes (Matthew 26:57–67; quote: NIV). These events were part of Jesus' suffering to pay for our sins.

What does this mean? We should fear and love God so that we do not tell lies about our neighbor, betray him, slander him, or hurt his reputation, but defend him, speak well of him, and explain everything in the kindest way.

King Saul hated David and planned to kill him. But Saul's son Jonathan and David were friends. Jonathan gave David gifts—clothes and a sword and belt. Jonathan talked with his father about David. Jonathan spoke well of David and defended him before Saul (1 Samuel 18:3–4; 19:1–4). Jonathan's love for his friend David reminds us of the love Jesus has for us. Jesus speaks before His heavenly Father on our behalf. He gave His very life to save us.

The Ninth Commandment

You shall not covet your neighbor's house.

Wicked King Ahab coveted the vineyard of a man named Naboth. When Naboth refused to sell it to him, the king sulked and brooded. Queen Jezebel came up with a plan. She told people to lie, saying Naboth had committed a crime. Accused of the crime, Naboth was put to death and Ahab received the vineyard. God was angry about the actions of Ahab and Jezebel. The lives of both came to a tragic end (1 Kings 21). Jesus calls us to repentance and offers forgiveness for all sins, including those involving coveting.

What does this mean? We should fear and love God so that we do not scheme to get our neighbor's inheritance or house, or get it in a way which only appears right, but help and be of service to him in keeping it.

Once some enemies came and carried away the people of the city of Sodom and many of their possessions. Among these people was Abraham's nephew Lot. After Abraham had rescued the people, the king of Sodom wanted to give Abraham the people's possessions as a reward. Abraham refused. He wanted the people to have all the items returned to them. Abraham gave God a tenth of all he had acquired in battle. He presented these things to Melchizedek, king of Jerusalem and priest of God (Genesis 14). Many years later, God sent His Son to rescue us; He gave us the greatest gift of all—salvation.

The Tenth Commandment

You shall not covet your neighbor's wife, or his manservant or maidservant, his ox or donkey, or anything that belongs to your neighbor.

Once King David looked out from his palace and saw a married woman named Bathsheba. David wanted her for his wife. He set into motion a plan to have Bathsheba's husband killed so he could marry her. But the Lord knew what David had done. He sent the prophet Nathan to tell David about a sinful man who had done a terrible thing. "You are that man," Nathan told David. David then realized the terrible things he had done. David repented and God forgave him. (2 Samuel 11:1–12:13)

What does this mean? We should fear and love God so that we do not entice or force away our neighbor's wife, workers, or animals, or turn them against him, but urge them to stay and do their duty.

Sarah, Abraham's wife, had a servant named Hagar. Hagar regarded Sarah disrespectfully and Sarah treated Hagar poorly in return. Finally Hagar ran away. But the angel of the Lord came to Hagar as she rested by a desert spring. "Go back to Sarah and submit to her," said the angel, "and God will bless you." Hagar did as the angel had said (Genesis 16). Many years later God sent Jesus to pay for the wrongs we do to one another. Jesus loves us and serves us and leads us to love, serve, and submit to one another.

The Close of the Commandments

What does God say about all these commandments?
He says: "I, the LORD your God, am a jealous God, punishing the children for the sin of the fathers to the third and fourth generation of those who hate Me, but showing love to a thousand generations of those who love Me and keep My commandments."
[Exodus 20:5–6 NIV]

Long ago, God looked down on the earth and considered how wickedly people treated one another. What God saw filled His heart with pain. Only Noah walked with God. God told Noah to build an ark. Into the ark God told Noah to assemble his family and two of every kind of animal. God sent a flood to destroy every living thing outside the ark. But God saved everything inside the ark, including Noah and his family (Genesis 6–7).

What does this mean? God threatens to punish all who break these commandments. Therefore, we should fear His wrath and not do anything against them. But He promises grace and every blessing to all who keep these commandments. Therefore, we should also love and trust in Him and gladly do what He commands.

When God sent a flood to destroy all He had made, only Noah and his family and the animals inside the ark remained safe. As the floodwaters receded, the ark landed on a mountaintop. Noah and his family left the ark and worshiped God. God placed a rainbow in the sky as a reminder of His grace and promises. Never again would God destroy the world with a flood. God blessed Noah and his descendants in the new life they had after the flood. (Genesis 8:1–9:17)

THE FIRST TABLE

"Love the Lord your God with all your heart and with all your soul and with all your mind" (Matthew 22:37 NIV).

The First Commandment

"You shall have no other gods" (Exodus 20:3 NIV).

The Second Commandment

"You shall not misuse the name of the Lord your God" (Exodus 20:7 NIV).

The Third Commandment

"Remember the Sabbath day by keeping it holy" (Exodus 20:8 NIV).

THE SECOND TABLE
"Love your neighbor as yourself"
(Matthew 22:39 NIV).

The Fourth Commandment

"Honor your father and your mother"
(Exodus 20:12 NIV).

The Fifth Commandment

"You shall not murder" (Exodus 20:13 NIV).

The Sixth Commandment

"You shall not commit adultery"
(Exodus 20:14 NIV).

The Seventh Commandment

"You shall not steal" (Exodus 20:15 NIV).

The Eighth Commandment

"You shall not give false testimony against your
neighbor" (Exodus 20:16 NIV).

The Ninth Commandment

"You shall not covet your neighbor's house"
(Exodus 20:17a NIV).

The Tenth Commandment

"You shall not covet your neighbor's wife, or his
manservant or maidservant, his ox or donkey, or
anything that belongs to your neighbor"
(Exodus 30:17b NIV).

The Apostles' Creed

As the head of the family
should teach it in a simple way
to his household

Long ago, at just the right time, God sent His Son, conceived by the Holy Spirit and born of the Virgin Mary, to be our Savior. Shortly after Jesus' birth, Wise Men from a distant land followed a star so that they might worship the Savior (Matthew 2:1–11). The true God is the Trinity—Father, Son, and Holy Spirit. There are three persons and only one God. This truth about God is very difficult to understand. Yet God gives spiritual wisdom to those who trust in Him. God loves us. He wants "all [people] to be saved and to come to a knowledge of the truth" (1 Timothy 2:4 NIV). God invites us all to come to Him in worship.

The First Article

CREATION

I believe in God, the Father Almighty, Maker of heaven and earth.

What does this mean? I believe that God has made me and all creatures; that He has given me my body and soul, eyes, ears, and all my members, my reason and all my senses, and still takes care of them.

He also gives me clothing and shoes, food and drink, house and home, wife and children, land, animals, and all I have. He richly and daily provides me with all that I need to support this body and life.

He defends me against all danger and guards and protects me from all evil.

All this He does only out of fatherly, divine goodness and mercy, without any merit or worthiness in me. For all this it is my duty to thank and praise, serve and obey Him.

This is most certainly true.

I believe in God, the Father Almighty, Maker of heaven and earth.

At the beginning of time, God made all things. He created the earth and all the planets, the sun, moon, and stars, all the trees and plants, fish, birds, creeping things, and all land animals. Finally, God made Adam and Eve, the first people. He gave them a beautiful home called the Garden of Eden. Adam and Eve were very happy. God made all of this in just six days. Then He rested. Everything God made was good. Unlike now, there was no sin in the world at its beginning (Genesis 1–2). Because we know Jesus as our Savior, one day we will have a wonderful home in heaven just like the Garden of Eden.

The Second Article

REDEMPTION

And in Jesus Christ, His only Son, our Lord, who was conceived by the Holy Spirit, born of the Virgin Mary, suffered under Pontius Pilate, was crucified, died and was buried. He descended into hell. The third day He rose again from the dead. He ascended into heaven and sits at the right hand of God, the Father Almighty. From thence He will come to judge the living and the dead.

What does this mean? I believe that Jesus Christ, true God, begotten of the Father from eternity, and also true man, born of the Virgin Mary, is my Lord,

who has redeemed me, a lost and condemned person, purchased and won me from all sins, from death, and from the power of the devil; not with gold or silver, but with His holy, precious blood and with His innocent suffering and death,

that I may be His own and live under Him in His kingdom and serve Him in everlasting righteousness, innocence, and blessedness,

just as He is risen from the dead, lives and reigns to all eternity.

This is most certainly true.

And in Jesus Christ His only Son, our Lord.

God sent Jesus to earth to live a holy life in our place and to die for our sins and the sins of all people. Both true God and true man, Jesus obeyed His heavenly Father perfectly in our place. He died in our place, taking our punishment upon Himself. Then He arose at Easter.

Who was conceived by the Holy Spirit.

One day the angel Gabriel appeared with an important message for a young woman named Mary. "You … are highly favored," he said. Gabriel told Mary that she would be the mother of God's Son, the promised Savior. Mary asked, "How can I be a mother?" Gabriel replied, "The Holy Spirit will come upon you and the power of the Most High will overshadow you. So the holy one to be born will be called the Son of God." "I am the Lord's servant," Mary said. "May it be to me as you have said." And then the angel left her. (Luke 1:26–38; quotes: NIV)

Born of the Virgin Mary.

Caesar Augustus required that family members return to their hometown for a census. Joseph and Mary traveled to Bethlehem because they were from the family of David. While they were there, Mary gave birth to the Savior of the world. She wrapped Him in cloths and laid Him in a manger. There was no room for them in the inn. Outside Bethlehem, shepherds were watching their flocks by night. Angels appeared to announce to them the Savior's birth. The shepherds hurried to Bethlehem and then told everyone the good news, "The Savior is born!" (Luke 2:1–20)

Suffered under Pontius Pilate.

Because of our sins, Jesus suffered horrible pain. Roman governor Pontius Pilate ordered his soldiers to whip Jesus. They twisted together a crown of thorns and put it on His head. Then they mocked Him. They dressed Jesus in a purple robe like kings wore and called, "Hail, king of the Jews!" And they slapped Him in His face. Pilate said, "I find no basis for a charge against Him." But the people yelled, "Crucify Him!" (John 19:1–6; Mark 15:1–15; quotes: NIV). Jesus endured this pain, humiliation, and suffering because He loves you and me.

Was crucified.

The soldiers led Jesus outside the city. Jesus carried His own cross to a place called Golgotha. Here they nailed Him to the cross and placed it into the ground. People mocked, sneered, and insulted Jesus. But from the cross Jesus forgave the criminal being crucified next to Him as well as those who were crucifying Him; asked John to care for Mary, His mother; asked for something to drink; spoke of God's forsaking Him because of our sins; and committed His spirit to God. Jesus said, "It is finished." Then He bowed His head and died for the sins of the world. (Matthew 27:32–56; Mark 15:25–37; Luke 23:33–46; John 19:17–30; quote: NIV)

Died and was buried.

Friends of Jesus, Joseph of Arimathea and Nicodemus, asked Pilate for the body of Jesus. With Pilate's permission they took Jesus' body and prepared it for burial. Wrapping Jesus' body together with burial spices, they placed it in a new tomb, located near the crucifixion site. Then they rolled a stone against the entrance to the tomb and went to their homes. (Matthew 27:57–60; Mark 15:42–46; Luke 23:50–56; John 19:38–42)

He descended into hell. The third day He rose again from the dead.

Hell is the place reserved for the devil and those who do not believe in Jesus as Savior. After His death, Jesus went to proclaim His victory to those in hell (1 Peter 3:18–19). Then Jesus rose from the dead. Early on Easter morning there was a violent earthquake, for the angel of the Lord came down from heaven and rolled the stone away from the entrance to the tomb. Later, women went to Jesus' tomb. The angel told them Jesus had risen from the dead. The women hurried away from the tomb, filled with joy. (Matthew 28:1–8; Mark 16:1–8; Luke 24:1–8)

He ascended into heaven and sits at the right hand of God, the Father Almighty.

For 40 days after His resurrection from the dead Jesus appeared to many people. One day Jesus led His disciples to a place near Bethany. As He lifted up His hands and blessed them, Jesus rose from the ground higher and higher into the heavens. Then a cloud covered Jesus and His disciples could see Him no more. Suddenly two angels appeared. They told them that Jesus would come back. One day soon Jesus will come back to take us to heaven. Meanwhile Jesus is in heaven at His Father's right hand. (Mark 16:19; Luke 24:50–51; Acts 1:6–11)

From thence He will come to judge the living and the dead.

God keeps every promise. From God's Word we know that Jesus will come again. He will judge all people. All people will see Jesus and will recognize Him as the Son of God and Savior of the world. Those who do not believe in Jesus will go to eternal punishment in hell with the devil and his evil angels. Those with faith will go to live with Jesus forever in the happiness of heaven as He has promised. (Revelation 1:7, 20:11–15)

The Third Article

SANCTIFICATION

I believe in the Holy Spirit, the holy Christian church, the communion of saints, the forgiveness of sins, the resurrection of the body, and the life everlasting. Amen.

What does this mean? I believe that I cannot by my own reason or strength believe in Jesus Christ, my Lord, or come to Him; but the Holy Spirit has called me by the Gospel, enlightened me with His gifts, sanctified and kept me in the true faith.

In the same way He calls, gathers, enlightens, and sanctifies the whole Christian church on earth, and keeps it with Jesus Christ in the one true faith.

In this Christian church He daily and richly forgives all my sins and the sins of all believers.

On the Last Day He will raise me and all the dead, and give eternal life to me and all believers in Christ.

This is most certainly true.

I believe in the Holy Spirit, the holy Christian church, the communion of saints.

Fifty days after Easter, at the feast of Pentecost, the Holy Spirit came upon God's people. A mighty wind blew and what appeared like tongues of fire separated and appeared on Jesus' followers. They began to speak in languages they had not learned. Peter preached a powerful sermon about Jesus. He told the people, "Repent and be baptized, every one of you, in the name of Jesus Christ for the forgiveness of your sins." About 3,000 people became believers that day. As the Christian church grew, the people came together often to learn and pray and to support and encourage one another. (Acts 2; quote: NIV)

The forgiveness of sins.

Jesus once told the story about a son who asked his father for his inheritance. The son went to a far country and wasted his money on parties. When his money was gone, the son was so poor he worked feeding pigs. He remembered how well his father's servants lived. The son decided to return home to ask his father to let him be a servant. But the father welcomed him home not as a servant but as a son. The father gave him fine clothes, jewelry, and a lavish celebration (Luke 15:11–24). In this same way Jesus forgives us with abundant grace as we repent of the wrong things we have done.

The resurrection of the body, and the life everlasting. Amen.

When Jesus comes again, the Holy Spirit will bring back to life all people who have ever lived. With our own eyes each of us will see Jesus, even if we have been dead for many years (Job 19:25–27). Jesus will change those who believe in Him (1 Corinthians 15:51–52). We will have glorified bodies. The change of a caterpillar into a butterfly reminds us of the change from death to new life. A crown reminds us of the joy and happiness Jesus will give us in heaven (Revelation 2:10).

The Apostles' Creed

I believe in God the Father Almighty, Maker of heaven and earth.

And in Jesus Christ, His only Son, our Lord, who was conceived by the Holy Spirit, born of the Virgin Mary, suffered under Pontius Pilate, was crucified, died and was buried. He descended into hell. The third day He rose again from the dead. He ascended into heaven and sits at the right hand of God, the Father Almighty. From thence He will come to judge the living and the dead.

I believe in the Holy Spirit, the holy Christian church, the communion of saints, the forgiveness of sins, the resurrection of the body, and the life everlasting. Amen.

The Lord's Prayer

AS THE HEAD OF THE FAMILY
SHOULD TEACH IT IN A SIMPLE WAY
TO HIS HOUSEHOLD

Jesus taught by what He said and did. Once, Jesus' disciples asked Him how they were to pray. Jesus taught them the Lord's Prayer (Matthew 6:9–13). Sometime later, before He did a miracle to feed thousands of people, Jesus looked up to heaven and gave thanks to His heavenly Father. Then He broke the loaves and fed the people (Matthew 14: 19b–21).

The Introduction

Our Father, who art in heaven.

We have a Father in heaven who loves us. He cares so much about us that He sent His only Son to earth to pay the penalty we deserve because of our sins. Our Father in heaven always wants what's best for us. God's Word asks, "Which of you, if his son asks for bread, will give him a stone? Or if he asks for a fish, will give him a snake? ... How much more will your Father in heaven give good gifts to those who ask Him!" (Matthew 7:9–11; quote: NIV)

What does this mean? With these words God tenderly invites us to believe that He is our true Father and that we are His true children, so that with all boldness and confidence we may ask Him as dear children ask their dear father.

Jesus taught His followers about His Father's love for all people. He invites us to call God our Father and to come to Him in prayer, confident of His care for us. Psalm 103:13 (NIV) reminds us, "As a father has compassion on his children, so the LORD has compassion on those who fear Him." The Apostle John wrote, "How great is the love the Father has lavished on us, that we should be called children of God! And that is what we are!" (1 John 3:1 NIV).

The First Petition
Hallowed be Thy name.

Jesus' disciples Peter, James, and John once got a glimpse of the holiness of God. Jesus took them to a high mountain. Suddenly Jesus' face and clothes became very bright. Then Old Testament prophets Moses and Elijah appeared and talked with Jesus about the salvation He would bring to the world. Then God spoke from heaven, "This is My Son, whom I love; with Him I am well pleased. Listen to Him!" (Matthew 17:1–5; quote: NIV)

What does this mean? God's name is certainly holy in itself, but we pray in this petition that it may be kept holy among us also.

How is God's name kept holy? God's name is kept holy when the Word of God is taught in its truth and purity, and we, as the children of God, also lead holy lives according to it. Help us to do this, dear Father in heaven! But anyone who teaches or lives contrary to God's Word profanes the name of God among us. Protect us from this, heavenly Father!

Jesus taught His disciples many things about God and His love. "Don't worry," Jesus said. "Look at the birds. They know your heavenly Father feeds them. Or, why worry about what you are going to wear? Look at the lilies of the field. They don't care about clothes. Yet see how beautiful they look. So don't worry about what you will eat or drink. God knows you need these things. Instead, seek God's kingdom and His righteousness and all these things will be given to you as well." (Matthew 6:25–33)

The Second Petition
Thy kingdom come.

Many years ago God's people did not associate with people of different cultures. One day God directed Peter to bring the Good News of Jesus to the Gentiles. That same day, men from another country arrived and invited Peter to go with them to their hometown, Caesarea. Peter went with them. He told the people there that Jesus died on the cross to take away their sins. Peter said, "Now I know that God does not show favoritism." Peter helped bring God's kingdom to the Gentiles. (Acts 10)

What does this mean? The kingdom of God certainly comes by itself without our prayer, but we pray in this petition that it may come to us also.

How does God's kingdom come? God's kingdom comes when our heavenly Father gives us His Holy Spirit, so that by His grace we believe His holy Word and lead godly lives here in time and there in eternity.

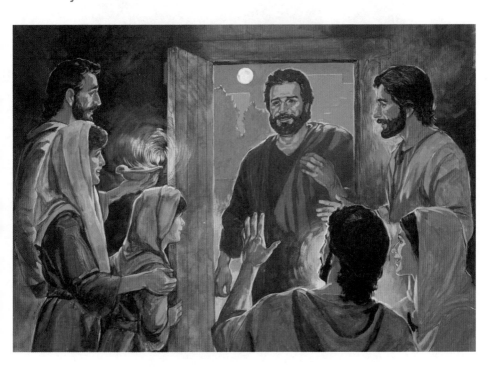

Paul and his friend Silas once crossed the sea to bring the Good News of Jesus to the people living there. Outside the city of Philippi they met a woman named Lydia. Lydia was a businesswoman who sold purple dye. The Lord opened Lydia's heart, and she became a follower of Jesus. When Lydia and her family were baptized, she invited Paul and Silas to stay at her house. (Acts 16:13–15)

The Third Petition

Thy will be done on earth as it is in heaven.

The night before He died on the cross for the sins of the world, Jesus went to the Garden of Gethsemane. There He prayed, "Father, if it is possible, take this cup of suffering away from Me. Yet, let not My will but Your will be done." Jesus prayed this same prayer three times. Then God sent an angel from heaven to strengthen Him. (Matthew 26:36–44; Luke 22:39–44)

What does this mean? The good and gracious will of God is done even without our prayer, but we pray in this petition that it may be done among us also.

How is God's will done? God's will is done when He breaks and hinders every evil plan and purpose of the devil, the world, and our sinful nature, which do not want us to hallow God's name or let His kingdom come; and when He strengthens and keeps us firm in His Word and faith until we die. This is His good and gracious will.

Paul, or Saul as he was first called, was once an enemy of the people of God. He threatened to kill the followers of Jesus. Saul was on his way to capture Christians in Damascus when suddenly a bright light from heaven shone on him. Falling to the ground he heard Jesus' voice saying, "Saul, Saul, why do you persecute Me?" Paul came to faith in Jesus as his Savior and was baptized. Then God told Paul His will for his life. Paul was to become a Christian missionary. He would travel throughout the world telling people about Jesus. (Acts 9:1–16; quote: NIV)

The Fourth Petition
Give us this day our daily bread.

God gives His people all they need to live and to enjoy living. Among His blessings are food, clothes, friends, fun times, and meaningful work. The Apostle Paul knew all of these blessings in his life. God gave him food and clothes. God also gave Paul good friends. Paul's friends Priscilla and Aquila spent time with him. They worked together making tents as they talked about Jesus, their best and truest friend. They told people about Jesus, the Savior. (Acts 18:1–4)

What does this mean? God certainly gives daily bread to everyone without our prayers, even to all evil people, but we pray in this petition that God would lead us to realize this and to receive our daily bread with thanksgiving.

What is meant by daily bread? Daily bread includes everything that has to do with the support and needs of the body, such as food, drink, clothing, shoes, house, home, land, animals, money, goods, a devout husband or wife, devout children, devout workers, devout and faithful rulers, good government, good weather, peace, health, self-control, good reputation, good friends, faithful neighbors, and the like.

When Jesus called His first disciples, He performed a miracle involving their work as fishermen. Jesus wanted the disciples to know that He would always take care of their daily needs. He told the disciples to go out into the deep water and let down their nets. The disciples caught so many fish their nets began to break. "From now on you will catch men," Jesus said. So the disciples left everything and followed Him. (Luke 5:1–11; quote: NIV)

The Fifth Petition

And forgive us our trespasses as we forgive those who trespass against us.

Once when Jesus was a dinner guest in someone's house, a woman who had lived a sinful life came up to Jesus. She began to cry. She washed Jesus' feet with her tears and dried them with her hair. Then she kissed Jesus' feet and poured perfume on them. Jesus said to the woman, "Your sins are forgiven." Then, "Your faith has saved you; go in peace." (Luke 7:36–50; quote: NIV)

What does this mean? We pray in this petition that our Father in heaven would not look at our sins, or deny our prayer because of them. We are neither worthy of the things for which we pray, nor have we deserved them, but we ask that He would give them all to us by grace, for we daily sin much and surely deserve nothing but punishment. So we too will sincerely forgive and gladly do good to those who sin against us.

Peter once asked Jesus, "Lord, how many times shall I forgive my brother when he sins against me? Up to seven times?" Jesus answered, "I tell you, not seven times, but seventy-seven times." Jesus wanted Peter to know the great extent of God's forgiveness (Matthew 18:21–22; quote: NIV). Later, Peter would experience God's full and complete forgiveness in a very personal way. God forgave Peter for denying he was Jesus' follower. God's forgiveness for us in Christ Jesus knows no limits. No sin is too great for God to forgive.

The Sixth Petition

And lead us not into temptation.

On the night of Jesus' arrest, Peter proclaimed that he would never disown Jesus. Later that night, Peter waited for news of the trial outside in courtyard. While he waited, a servant girl pointed Peter out as a follower of Jesus. Peter denied it. When another girl made the same observation, Peter denied it again, this time with an oath. At the third accusation, Peter began to curse and swear, saying, "I don't know the man!" Then, remembering Jesus' warning and realizing what he had done, Peter left and wept bitterly. (Matthew 26:69–75; quote: NIV)

What does this mean? God tempts no one. We pray in this petition that God would guard and keep us so that the devil, the world, and our sinful nature may not deceive us or mislead us into false belief, despair, and other great shame and vice. Although we are attacked by these things, we pray that we may finally overcome them and win the victory.

Job, a faithful follower of the true God, lived in the land of Uz. Satan brought Job much misery and torment. Satan tempted Job to curse God. When Job had lost almost everything, Satan brought sickness into Job's life. Job was covered with boils from head to foot. Job might have cursed God, but he didn't. Instead, he trusted God. God helped Job to resist temptation. (Job 1–2)

The Seventh Petition
But deliver us from evil.

Once a Canaanite woman begged Jesus to heal her daughter. Jesus remained quiet and the disciples urged Him to send her away. But the woman didn't give up. Then Jesus said, "It is not right to give the children's bread to the dogs." The woman agreed but added that dogs sometimes do get to eat the food that falls from the master's table. Jesus granted the woman's request. "Your faith is great!" He said (Matthew 15:21–28). God wants us to ask Him to protect us from all sickness and pain, harm and danger, and all other evils. He has the power to help us in the way He knows is best.

What does this mean? We pray in this petition, in summary, that our Father in heaven would rescue us from every evil of body and soul, possessions and reputation, and finally, when our last hour comes, give us a blessed end, and graciously take us from this valley of sorrow to Himself in heaven.

Jesus once told a story about a rich man and a poor man. While the rich man lived in luxury, the poor beggar, named Lazarus, lay sick and hungry at his gate. Both died. The angels carried Lazarus to heaven. The rich man died and went to hell. Now everything was changed. Lazarus knew the comfort and happiness of heaven. But the rich man lived in pain and agony without even any water to cool his tongue (Luke 16:19–31). Heaven is God's gift, received by faith by those who trust in Jesus as their Savior.

The Conclusion

For Thine is the kingdom and the power and the glory forever and ever.* Amen.

What does this mean? This means that I should be certain that these petitions are pleasing to our Father in heaven, and are heard by Him; for He Himself has commanded us to pray in this way and has promised to hear us. Amen, amen means "yes, yes, it shall be so."

Writing by inspiration of the Holy Spirit, the Apostle John provides us with a glimpse of heaven. Thousands upon thousands of angels circle the heavenly throne singing praises to Jesus. In a loud voice they glorify Jesus for the salvation He brings to God's people. The angels sing, "Worthy is the lamb, who was slain, to receive power and wealth and wisdom and strength and honor and glory and praise!" (Revelation 5:11–12). Jesus is the victorious Lamb of God who died to take away our sins. Praise God that He gives His victory to us! (1 Corinthians 15:57)

*These words were not in Luther's Small Catechism.

Our Father who art in heaven, hallowed be Thy name, Thy kingdom come, Thy will be done on earth as it is in heaven. Give us this day our daily bread; and forgive us our trespasses as we forgive those who trespass against us; and lead us not into temptation, but deliver us from evil. For Thine is the kingdom and the power and the glory forever and ever. Amen.

Our Father in heaven, hallowed be Your name, Your kingdom come, Your will be done on earth as in heaven. Give us today our daily bread. Forgive us our sins as we forgive those who sin against us. Lead us not into temptation, but deliver us from evil. For the kingdom, the power, and the glory are Yours now and forever. Amen.

The Sacrament of Holy Baptism

As the head of the family
should teach it in a simple way
to his household

In the name of the Father and of the Son and of the Holy Spirit.

God has given Baptism as a gift to His people. Through Baptism, by faith, God works forgiveness of sins, new life, and salvation. In Baptism each of us joins the family of God. "For we were all baptized by one Spirit into one body—whether Jews or Greeks, slave or free" (1 Corinthians 12:13 NIV).

THE SACRAMENT OF HOLY BAPTISM

FIRST

What is Baptism?

Baptism is not just plain water, but it is the water included in God's command and combined with God's word.

Jesus came from Galilee to the river Jordan to be baptized by John. As soon as Jesus was baptized, He came out of the water. Just then, heaven was opened and He saw God the Holy Spirit descending like a dove and landing on Him. And God the Father spoke from heaven, "This is My Son, whom I love; with Him I am well pleased." (Matthew 3:13–17; quote: NIV)

Which is that word of God?

Christ our Lord says in the last chapter of Matthew: "Therefore go and make disciples of all nations, baptizing them in the name of the Father and of the Son and of the Holy Spirit." [Matthew 28:19 NIV]

After Jesus' resurrection from the dead, the disciples worshiped Jesus on a mountain in the region of Galilee. Jesus said to them, "All authority in heaven and on earth has been given to Me. Therefore go and make disciples of all nations, baptizing them in the name of the Father and of the Son and of the Holy Spirit, and teaching them to obey everything I have commanded you. And surely I am with you always, to the very end of the age." (Matthew 28:16–20; quote: NIV)

Second

What benefits does Baptism give?

It works forgiveness of sins, rescues from death and the devil, and gives eternal salvation to all who believe this, as the words and promises of God declare.

People were bringing little children to Jesus to have Him pray for them. When the disciples tried to keep the children away, Jesus was displeased with the disciples. He said, "Let the little children come to Me, and do not hinder them, for the kingdom of heaven belongs to such as these." (Matthew 19:13–14; quote: NIV)

Which are these words and promises of God?

Christ our Lord says in the last chapter of Mark: "Whoever believes and is baptized will be saved, but whoever does not believe will be condemned." [Mark 16:16 NIV]

An important official in charge of the treasury of Candace, the queen of Ethiopia, was reading from the book of Isaiah as he traveled home in his chariot. The Ethiopian official read Isaiah's words about a lamb that was killed. A man of God named Philip was also traveling down the road. He told the Ethiopian that the lamb Isaiah wrote about was Jesus, who died for the sins of the world, and the Ethiopian believed. When they came to some water, the Ethiopian asked to be baptized. After Philip baptized him, the man rejoiced as he went on his way. (Acts 8:26–40)

THIRD

How can water do such great things?

Certainly not just water, but the word of God in and with the water does these things, along with the faith which trusts this word of God in the water. For without God's word the water is plain water and no Baptism. But with the word of God it is a Baptism, that is, a life-giving water, rich in grace, and a washing of the new birth in the Holy Spirit.

Nicodemus, a Pharisee, came to talk with Jesus one night. Jesus told him, "No one can enter the kingdom of God without being born again." "How can an old person be born again?" Nicodemus asked. Jesus replied, "No one can enter God's kingdom without first being born by water and God's Spirit. People give birth to people, but God's Spirit gives birth to our spirit." Jesus told Nicodemus that whoever believes in Him shall not perish but have eternal life. (John 3:1–16)

As St. Paul says in Titus, chapter three:

"He saved us through the washing of rebirth and renewal by the Holy Spirit, whom He poured out on us generously through Jesus Christ our Savior, so that, having been justified by His grace, we might become heirs having the hope of eternal life. This is a trustworthy saying." [Titus 3:5–8 NIV]

FOURTH

What does such baptizing with water indicate?

It indicates that the Old Adam in us should by daily contrition and repentance be drowned and die with all sins and evil desires, and that a new man should daily emerge and arise to live before God in righteousness and purity forever.

Where is this written?

St. Paul writes in Romans chapter six: "We were therefore buried with Him through baptism into death in order that, just as Christ was raised from the dead through the glory of the Father, we too may live a new life." [Romans 6:4 NIV]

Rescue me from my enemies, O LORD, for I hide myself
in You. . . . For Your name's sake, O LORD, preserve my life;
in Your righteousness, bring me out of trouble.
(Psalm 143:9–11 NIV)

Confession

How christians should be taught to confess

What is confession?

First, that we confess our sins, and

second, that we receive absolution, that is, forgiveness, from the pastor as from God Himself, not doubting, but firmly believing that by it our sins are forgiven before God in heaven.

What sins should we confess?

Before God we should plead guilty of all sins, even those we are not aware of, as we do in the Lord's Prayer; but before the pastor we should confess only those sins which we know and feel in our hearts.

Jesus once told about two men who went to the temple to pray. The Pharisee prayed, "God, I thank You that I am not like other men—robbers, evildoers, adulterers—or even like this tax collector." The tax collector simply prayed, "God, have mercy on me, a sinner." This man went home with his sins forgiven. (Luke 18:9–14; quotes: NIV)

Which are these?

Consider your place in life according to the Ten Commandments: Are you a father, mother, son, daughter, husband, wife, or worker? Have you been disobedient, unfaithful, or lazy? Have you been hot-tempered, rude, or quarrelsome? Have you hurt someone by your words or deeds? Have you stolen, been negligent, wasted anything, or done any harm?

Once King David had committed a terrible sin. David said to Nathan, God's prophet, "I have sinned against the LORD." Nathan replied, "The LORD has taken away your sin" (2 Samuel 12:13; quotes: NIV). David wrote and sang many songs thanking and praising God for His forgiving love. Many of these songs are included in the Book of Psalms in the Bible.

A SHORT FORM OF CONFESSION

The penitent says:

Dear confessor, I ask you please to hear my confession and to pronounce forgiveness in order to fulfill God's will.

I, a poor sinner, plead guilty before God of all sins. In particular I confess before you that as a servant, maid, etc. I, sad to say, serve my master unfaithfully, for in this and that I have not done what I was told to do. I have made him angry and caused him to curse. I have been negligent and allowed damage to be done.

Reflecting on God's grace and goodness, Jacob once humbly praised God with these words, "I am unworthy of all the kindness and faithfulness You have shown Your servant" (Genesis 32:10 NIV).

I have also been offensive in words and deeds. I have quarreled with my peers. I have grumbled about the lady of the house and cursed her. I am sorry for all of this and I ask for grace. I want to do better.

A master or lady of the house may say:

In particular I confess before you that I have not faithfully guided my children, servants, and wife to the glory of God. I have cursed. I have set a bad example by indecent words and deeds. I have hurt my neighbor and spoken evil of him. I have overcharged, sold inferior merchandise, and given less than was paid for.

[Let the penitent confess whatever else he has done against God's commandments and his own position.]

If, however, someone does not find himself burdened with these or greater sins, he should not trouble himself or search for or invent other sins, and thereby make confession a torture. Instead, he should mention one or two that he knows: In particular I confess that I have cursed; I have used improper words; I have neglected this or that, etc. Let that be enough.

But if you know of none at all (which hardly seems possible), then mention none in particular, but receive the forgiveness upon the general confession which you make to God before the confessor.

Then the confessor shall say:

God be merciful to you and strengthen your faith. Amen.

Furthermore:

Do you believe that my forgiveness is God's forgiveness?

Yes, dear confessor.

Then let him say:

Let it be done for you as you believe. And I, by the command of our Lord Jesus Christ, forgive you your sins in the name of the Father and of the Son and of the Holy Spirit. Amen. Go in peace.

A confessor will know additional passages with which to comfort and to strengthen the faith of those who have great burdens of conscience or are sorrowful and distressed.

This is intended only as a general form of confession.

THE OFFICE OF THE KEYS

*What is the Office of the Keys?**

The Office of the Keys is that special authority which Christ has given to His church on earth to forgive the sins of repentant sinners, but to withhold forgiveness from the unrepentant as long as they do not repent.

*Where is this written?**

This is what St. John the Evangelist writes in chapter twenty: The Lord Jesus breathed on His disciples and said, "Receive the Holy Spirit. If you forgive anyone his sins, they are forgiven; if you do not forgive them, they are not forgiven." [John 20:22–23 NIV]

*What do you believe according to these words?**

I believe that when the called ministers of Christ deal with us by His divine command, in particular when they exclude openly unrepentant sinners from the Christian congregation and absolve those who repent of their sins and want to do better, this is just as valid and certain, even in heaven, as if Christ our dear Lord dealt with us Himself.

*This question may not have been composed by Luther himself but reflects his teaching and was included in editions of the catechism during his lifetime.

On the evening of the day of His resurrection from the dead, Jesus appeared to His disciples while they were together in a locked room. He stood among them and said, "Peace be with you!" Then Jesus showed them His hands and side. The disciples were overjoyed! Then Jesus said, "As the Father has sent Me, I am sending you. Receive the Holy Spirit. If you forgive anyone his sins, they are forgiven; if you do not forgive them, they are not forgiven." (John 20:19–23; quotes: NIV)

The Sacrament
of the Altar

As THE HEAD OF THE FAMILY
SHOULD TEACH IT IN A SIMPLE WAY
TO HIS HOUSEHOLD

The Lord Jesus, on the night He was betrayed, took bread, and when He had given thanks, He broke it and said, "This is My body, which is for you; do this in remembrance of Me." In the same way, after supper He took the cup, saying "This cup is the new covenant in My blood; do this, whenever you drink it, in remembrance of Me." For whenever you eat this bread and drink this cup, you proclaim the Lord's death until He comes. (1 Corinthians 11:23b–26 NIV)

What is the Sacrament of the Altar?

It is the true body and blood of our Lord Jesus Christ under the bread and wine, instituted by Christ Himself for us Christians to eat and to drink.

The night before His death, Jesus shared the Passover meal with His disciples. During the meal, Jesus took some bread, gave thanks, broke the bread, and gave it to His disciples, saying, "Take and eat; this is My body." Then He took the cup, gave thanks, and offered it to them as He said, "Drink from it, all of you. This is My blood of the [new] covenant, which is poured out for many for the forgiveness of sins." (Matthew 26:26–28; quotes: NIV)

Where is this written?

The holy Evangelists Matthew, Mark, Luke, and St. Paul write:

Our Lord Jesus Christ, on the night when He was betrayed, took bread, and when He had given thanks, He broke it and gave it to the disciples and said: "Take, eat; this is My body, which is given for you. This do in remembrance of Me."

In the same way also He took the cup after supper, and when He had given thanks, He gave it to them, saying, "Drink of it, all of you; this cup is the new testament in My blood, which is shed for you for the forgiveness of sins. This do, as often as you drink it, in remembrance of Me."

What is the benefit of this eating and drinking?

These words, "Given and shed for you for the forgiveness of sins," show us that in the Sacrament forgiveness of sins, life, and salvation are given us through these words. For where there is forgiveness of sins, there is also life and salvation.

How can bodily eating and drinking do such great things?

Certainly not just eating and drinking do these things, but the words written here: "Given and shed for you for the forgiveness of sins." These words, along with the bodily eating and drinking, are the main thing in the Sacrament. Whoever believes these words has exactly what they say: "forgiveness of sins."

"For whenever you eat this bread and drink this cup, you proclaim the Lord's death until He comes" (1 Corinthians 11:26 NIV).

Who receives this sacrament worthily?

Fasting and bodily preparation are certainly fine outward training. But that person is truly worthy and well prepared who has faith in these words: "Given and shed for you for the forgiveness of sins." But anyone who does not believe these words or doubts them is unworthy and unprepared, for the words "for you" require all hearts to believe.

When His people were slaves in Egypt, God told each household to prepare a special lamb, which was to be without defect. The people were to cook and eat the lamb and to spread the lamb's blood on the doorframe of their home. On Passover night the angel of the Lord passed over the land killing the firstborn in every house that didn't have blood on the doorframe. After the Passover, Pharaoh commanded God's people to leave Egypt. And so God delivered His people from slavery (Exodus 12:1–42). God delivers us from the slavery of sin through the blood of Jesus.

Daily Prayers

How the head of the family should teach his household to pray morning and evening

Morning Prayer

In the morning when you get up, make the sign of the holy cross and say:

In the name of the Father and of the Son and of the Holy Spirit. Amen.

Then, kneeling or standing, repeat the Creed and the Lord's Prayer. If you choose, you may also say this little prayer:

I thank You, my heavenly Father, through Jesus Christ, Your dear Son, that You have kept me this night from all harm and danger; and I pray that You would keep me this day also from sin and every evil, that all my doings and life may please You. For into Your hands I commend myself, my body and soul, and all things. Let Your holy angel be with me, that the evil foe may have no power over me. Amen.

Then go joyfully to your work, singing a hymn, like that of the Ten Commandments, or whatever your devotion may suggest.

Evening Prayer

In the evening when you go to bed, make the sign of the holy cross and say:

In the name of the Father and of the Son and of the Holy Spirit. Amen.

Then kneeling or standing, repeat the Creed and the Lord's Prayer. If you choose you may also say this little prayer:

I thank You, my heavenly Father, through Jesus Christ, Your dear Son, that You have graciously kept me this day; and I pray that You would forgive me all my sins where I have done wrong, and graciously keep me this night. For into Your hands I commend myself, my body and soul, and all things. Let Your holy angel be with me, that the evil foe may have no power over me. Amen.

Then go to sleep at once and in good cheer.

HOW THE HEAD OF THE FAMILY
SHOULD TEACH HIS HOUSEHOLD
TO ASK A BLESSING AND RETURN THANKS

Asking a Blessing

The children and members of the household shall go to the table reverently, fold their hands, and say:

The eyes of all look to You, [O Lord,] and You give them their food at the proper time. You open Your hand and satisfy the desires of every living thing. [Psalm 145:15–16 NIV]

Then shall be said the Lord's Prayer and the following:

Lord God, heavenly Father, bless us and these Your gifts which we receive from Your bountiful goodness, through Jesus Christ, our Lord. Amen.

Returning Thanks

Also, after eating, they shall, in like manner, reverently and with folded hands say:

Give thanks to the Lord, for He is good. His love endures forever. [He] gives food to every creature. He provides food for the cattle and for the young ravens when they call. His pleasure is not in the strength of the horse, nor His delight in the legs of a man; the Lord delights in those who fear Him, who put their hope in His unfailing love. [Psalm 136:1, 25; 147:9–11 NIV]

Then shall be said the Lord's Prayer and the following:

We thank You, Lord God, heavenly Father, for all Your benefits, through Jesus Christ, our Lord, who lives and reigns with You and the Holy Spirit forever and ever. Amen.

Table of Duties

CERTAIN PASSAGES OF SCRIPTURE
FOR VARIOUS HOLY ORDERS AND
POSITIONS, ADMONISHING THEM ABOUT
THEIR DUTIES AND RESPONSIBILITIES

To Bishops, Pastors, and Preachers

The overseer must be above reproach, the husband of but one wife, temperate, self-controlled, respectable, hospitable, able to teach, not given to drunkenness, not violent but gentle, not quarrelsome, not a lover of money. He must manage his own family well and see that his children obey him with proper respect. (1 Timothy 3:2–4 NIV)

He must not be a recent convert, or he may become conceited and fall under the same judgment as the devil. (1 Timothy 3:6 NIV)

He must hold firmly to the trustworthy message as it has been taught, so that he can encourage others by sound doctrine and refute those who oppose it. (Titus 1:9 NIV)

What the Hearers Owe Their Pastors

The Lord has commanded that those who preach the gospel should receive their living from the gospel. (1 Corinthians 9:14 NIV)

Anyone who receives instruction in the word must share all good things with his instructor. Do not be deceived: God cannot be mocked. A man reaps what he sows. (Galatians 6:6–7 NIV)

The elders who direct the affairs of the church well are worthy of double honor, especially those whose work is preaching and teaching. For the Scripture says, "Do not muzzle the ox while it is treading out the grain," and "The worker deserves his wages." (1 Timothy 5:17–18 NIV)

We ask you, brothers, to respect those who work hard among you, who are over you in the Lord and who admonish you. Hold them in the highest regard in love because of their work. Live in peace with each other. (1 Thessalonians 5:12–13 NIV)

Obey your leaders and submit to their authority. They keep watch over you as men who must give an account. Obey them so that their work will be a joy, not a burden, for that would be of no advantage to you. (Hebrews 13:17 NIV)

Not knowing whether he would ever see them again, Paul met with the elders of the church at Ephesus. He reminded them of his ministry among them. Paul said, "I have declared to both Jews and Greeks that they must turn to God in repentance and have faith in our Lord Jesus." Then Paul and the elders prayed together and the elders accompanied Paul to the ship that would take him away. (Acts 20:17–38; quote: NIV)

Of Civil Government

Everyone must submit himself to the governing authorities, for there is no authority except that which God has established. The authorities that exist have been established by God. Consequently, he who rebels against the authority is rebelling against what God has instituted, and those who do so will bring judgment on themselves. For rulers hold no terror for those who do right, but for those who do wrong. Do you want to be free from fear of the one in authority? Then do what is right and he will commend you. For he is God's servant to do you good. But if you do wrong, be afraid, for he does not bear the sword for nothing. He is God's servant, an agent of wrath to bring punishment on the wrongdoer. (Romans 13:1–4 NIV)

Of Citizens

Give to Caesar what is Caesar's, and to God what is God's. (Matthew 22:21 NIV)

It is necessary to submit to the authorities, not only because of possible punishment but also because of conscience. This is also why you pay taxes, for the authorities are God's servants, who give their full time to governing. Give everyone what you owe him: If you owe taxes, pay taxes; if revenue, then revenue; if respect, then respect; if honor, then honor. (Romans 13:5–7 NIV)

I urge, then, first of all, that requests, prayers, intercession and thanksgiving be made for everyone—for kings and all those in authority, that we may live peaceful and quiet lives in all godliness and holiness. This is good, and pleases God our Savior. (1 Timothy 2:1–3 NIV)

Remind the people to be subject to rulers and authorities, to be obedient, to be ready to do whatever is good. (Titus 3:1 NIV)

Submit yourselves for the Lord's sake to every authority instituted among men: whether to the king, as the supreme authority, or to governors, who are sent by him to punish those who do wrong and to commend those who do right. (1 Peter 2:13–14 NIV)

The Apostle Paul had a young friend named Timothy. Timothy's grandmother Lois and his mother Eunice loved Jesus and trusted in Him for salvation (1 Timothy 1:5). Paul once reminded Timothy, "From infancy you have known the holy Scriptures, which are able to make you wise for salvation through faith in Christ Jesus" (2 Timothy 3:15 NIV). Those who trust in Jesus love to teach their children and grandchildren God's Word so that they learn and remember it. They love to tell others that Jesus loves them.

To Husbands

Husbands, in the same way be considerate as you live with your wives, and treat them with respect as the weaker partner and as heirs with you of the gracious gift of life, so that nothing will hinder your prayers. (1 Peter 3:7 NIV)

Husbands, love your wives and do not be harsh with them. (Colossians 3:19 NIV)

To Wives

Wives, submit to your husbands as to the Lord. (Ephesians 5:22 NIV)

They were submissive to their own husbands, like Sarah, who obeyed Abraham and called him her master. You are her daughters if you do what is right and do not give way to fear. (1 Peter 3:5–6 NIV)

To Parents

Fathers, do not exasperate your children; instead, bring them up in the training and instruction of the Lord. (Ephesians 6:4 NIV)

To Children

Children, obey your parents in the Lord, for this is right. "Honor your father and mother"—which is the first commandment with a promise—"that it may go well with you and that you may enjoy long life on the earth." (Ephesians 6:1–3 NIV)

To Workers of All Kinds

Slaves, obey your earthly masters with respect and fear, and with sincerity of heart, just as you would obey Christ. Obey them not only to win their favor when their eye is on you, but like slaves of Christ, doing the will of God from your heart. Serve wholeheartedly, as if you were serving the Lord, not men, because you know that the Lord will reward everyone for whatever good he does, whether he is slave or free. (Ephesians 6:5–8 NIV)

To Employers and Supervisors

Masters, treat your slaves in the same way. Do not threaten them, since you know that he who is both their Master and yours is in heaven, and there is no favoritism with Him. (Ephesians 6:9 NIV)

To Youth

Young men, in the same way be submissive to those who are older. All of you, clothe yourselves with humility toward one another, because, "God opposes the proud but gives grace to the humble." Humble yourselves, therefore, under God's mighty hand, that He may lift you up in due time. (1 Peter 5:5–6 NIV)

To Widows

The widow who is really in need and left all alone puts her hope in God and continues night and day to pray and to ask God for help. But the widow who lives for pleasure is dead even while she lives. (1 Timothy 5:5–6 NIV)

To Everyone

The commandments . . . are summed up in this one rule: "Love your neighbor as yourself." (Romans 13:9 NIV)

I urge . . . that requests, prayers, intercession and thanksgiving be made for everyone. (1 Timothy 2:1 NIV)

Let each his lesson learn with care,
and all the household well shall fare.

Christian Questions with Their Answers*

PREPARED BY DR. MARTIN LUTHER
FOR THOSE WHO INTEND TO GO
TO THE SACRAMENT

1. *Do you believe that you are a sinner?*

Yes, I believe it. I am a sinner.

2. *How do you know this?*

From the Ten Commandments, which I have not kept.

3. *Are you sorry for your sins?*

Yes, I am sorry that I have sinned against God.

4. *What have you deserved from God because of your sins?*

His wrath and displeasure, temporal death, and eternal damnation. See Romans 6:21, 23.

5. *Do you hope to be saved?*

Yes, that is my hope.

6. *In whom then do you trust?*

In my dear Lord Jesus Christ.

7. *Who is Christ?*

The Son of God, true God and man.

8. *How many Gods are there?*

Only one, but there are three persons: Father, Son, and Holy Spirit.

9. *What has Christ done for you that you trust in Him?*

He died for me and shed His blood for me on the cross for the forgiveness of sins.

10. *Did the Father also die for you?*

He did not. The Father is God only, as is the Holy Spirit; but the Son is both true God and true man. He died for me and shed His blood for me.

11. *How do you know this?*

From the holy Gospel, from the words instituting the Sacrament, and by His body and blood given me as a pledge in the Sacrament.

*The "Christian Questions with Their Answers," designating Luther as the author, first appeared in an edition of the Small Catechism in 1551.

12. *What are the words of institution?*

Our Lord Jesus Christ, on the night when He was betrayed, took bread, and when He had given thanks, He broke it and gave it to the disciples and said: "Take eat: this is My body, which is given for you. This do in remembrance of Me."

In the same way also He took the cup after supper, and when He had given thanks, He gave it to them, saying: "Drink of it, all of you; this cup is the new testament in My blood, which is shed for you for the forgiveness of sins. This do, as often as you drink it, in remembrance of Me."

13. *Do you believe, then, that the true body and blood of Christ are in the Sacrament?*

Yes, I believe it.

14. *What convinces you to believe this?*

The word of Christ: Take, eat, this is My body; drink of it, all of you, this is My blood.

15. *What should we do when we eat His body and drink His blood, and in this way receive His pledge?*

We should remember and proclaim His death and the shedding of His blood, as He taught us: This do, as often as you drink it, in remembrance of Me.

16. *Why should we remember and proclaim His death?*

First, so we may learn to believe that no creature could make satisfaction for our sins. Only Christ, true God and man, could do that. Second, so we may learn to be horrified by our sins, and to regard them as very serious. Third, so we may find joy and comfort in Christ alone, and through faith in Him be saved.

17. *What motivated Christ to die and make full payment for your sins?*

His great love for His Father and for me and other sinners, as it is written in John 14; Romans 5; Galatians 2 and Ephesians 5.

18. *Finally, why do you wish to go to the Sacrament?*

That I may learn to believe that Christ, out of great love, died for my sin, and also learn from Him to love God and my neighbor.

19. *What should admonish and encourage a Christian to receive the Sacrament frequently?*

First, both the command and the promise of Christ the Lord. Second, his own pressing need, because of which the command, encouragement, and promise are given.

20. *But what should you do if you are not aware of this need and have no hunger and thirst for the Sacrament?*

To such a person no better advice can be given then this: first, he should touch his body to see if he still has flesh and blood. Then he should believe what the Scriptures say of it in Galatians 5 and Romans 7.

Second, he should look around to see whether he is still in the world, and remember that there will be no lack of sin and trouble, as the Scriptures say in John 15–16 and in 1 John 2 and 5.

Third, he will certainly have the devil also around him, who with his lying and murdering day and night will let him have no peace, within or without, as the Scriptures picture him in John 8 and 16; 1 Peter 5; Ephesians 6; and 2 Timothy 2.

NOTE

These questions and answers are no child's play, but are drawn up with great earnestness of purpose by the venerable and devout Dr. Luther for both young and old. Let each one pay attention and consider it a serious matter; for St. Paul writes to the Galatians in chapter six: "Do not be deceived: God cannot be mocked" [Galatians 6:7 NIV].

Books of the Bible

BOOKS OF THE OLD TESTAMENT

Historical Books
The Pen'ta-teuch
(Five Books of Moses)

Gen'e-sis
Ex'o-dus
Le-vit'i-cus
Num'bers
Deu-ter-on'o-my
Josh'u-a
Judg'es
Ruth
1 Sam'u-el
2 Sam'u-el
1 Kings
2 Kings
1 Chron'i-cles
2 Chron'i-cles
Ez'ra
Ne-he-mi'ah
Esther

Poetic Books

Job
Psalms
Proverbs
Ec-cle-si-as'tes
Song of Songs

Prophetic Books
Major Prophets

I-sa'iah
Jer-e-mi'ah
Lam-en-ta'tions
E-ze'kiel
Dan'iel

Minor Prophets

Ho-se'a
Jo'el
A'mos
O-ba-di'ah
Jo'nah
Mi'cah
Na'hum
Hab-ak'kuk
Zeph-a-ni'ah
Hag'gai
Zech-a-ri'ah
Mal'a-chi

BOOKS OF THE NEW TESTAMENT

Historical Books

Mat'thew
Mark
Luke
John
Acts

Epistles

Ro'mans
1 Co-rin'thi-ans
2 Co-rin'thi-ans
Ga-la'tians
E-phe'sians
Phi-lip'pi-ans
Co-los'sians
1 Thes-sa-lo'nians
2 Thes-sa-lo'nians

1 Tim'o-thy
2 Tim'o-thy
Ti'tus
Phi-le'mon
He'brews
James
1 Pe'ter
2 Pe'ter
1 John
2 John
3 John
Jude

Prophetic Book

Rev-e-la'tion

Creeds and Confessions

In addition to the Apostles' Creed, the Nicene Creed, which is confessed at celebrations of the Lord's Supper, and the Athanasian Creed, often read on Holy Trinity Sunday, are universal statements of faith held by the Lutheran Church. Both concentrate especially on the person and work of Jesus Christ.

The Lutheran Church also accepts without reservation all the documents contained in *The Book of Concord* of 1580 as a true and unadulterated statement and exposition of the Word of God. The best known and most widely used of these is Dr. Martin Luther's Small Catechism.

Luther's Small Catechism and his Large Catechism, completed in 1529, were originally intended to be helpful manuals for pastors and family heads in teaching God's Word to children and adults. The Large Catechism is not made up of questions and answers but presents basic Christian teachings in a form often used in sermons.

Another well-known statement of faith, the Augsburg Confession, was written by Philip Melanchthon and read before Emperor Charles V at Augsburg, Germany, in 1530. While friendly in tone, it was adopted as a testimony against abuses prevalent in the church and against the errors of certain reformers regarding such crucial doctrines as original sin and the sacraments.

In 1531 Melanchthon wrote the Apology (Defense) of the Augsburg Confession. It too became an official confession of faith among Lutherans by its adoption at Smalcald, Germany, in 1537. In great detail it answers criticisms of the Augsburg Confession. Virtually half of the Apology is devoted to the Biblical doctrine of justification by grace through faith in Jesus Christ.

The Smalcald Articles were written by Luther in 1536 and signed by many clergy present at Smalcald in 1537. The Articles are a summary of Luther's main disagreements with the Roman Church. Melanchthon's Treatise on the Power and Primacy of the Pope was also officially adopted at Smalcald.

The Formula of Concord, completed in 1577, served to resolve doctrinal differences among Lutherans and was approved by over 8,000 theologians, pastors, and teachers by 1580. It was not a new confession but an exposition and defense of the previously adopted writings.

Quotations from these writings are included in this explanation of the Small Catechism.

The Church Year

Sundays and Major Festivals

The Time of Christmas

Advent Season
First Sunday in Advent
Second Sunday in Advent
Third Sunday in Advent
Fourth Sunday in Advent

Christmas Season
The Nativity of Our Lord
   Christmas Eve
   Christmas Dawn
   Christmas Day
First Sunday after Christmas
Second Sunday after Christmas

Epiphany Season
The Epiphany of Our Lord
The Baptism of Our Lord
   First Sunday after the Epiphany
Second Sunday after the Epiphany
Third Sunday after the Epiphany
Fourth Sunday after the Epiphany
Fifth Sunday after the Epiphany
Sixth Sunday after the Epiphany
Seventh Sunday after the Epiphany
Eighth Sunday after the Epiphany
The Transfiguration of Our Lord
   Last Sunday after the Epiphany

The Time of Easter

Lenten Season
Ash Wednesday
First Sunday in Lent

Good Friday

Second Sunday in Lent
Third Sunday in Lent
Fourth Sunday in Lent
Fifth Sunday in Lent

Holy Week
Palm Sunday
  Sunday of the Passion
Monday in Holy Week
Tuesday in Holy Week
Wednesday in Holy Week
Maundy Thursday
Good Friday

Easter Season
The Resurrection of Our Lord
  Easter Eve
  Easter Day
  Easter Evening
Second Sunday of Easter
Third Sunday of Easter
Fourth Sunday of Easter
Fifth Sunday of Easter
Sixth Sunday of Easter
The Ascension of Our Lord
Seventh Sunday of Easter
Pentecost
  Pentecost Eve
  The Day of Pentecost
  Pentecost Evening

The First Easter

The Time of the Church

The Season of Pentecost
The Holy Trinity
  First Sunday after Pentecost
Second through Twenty-seventh Sunday after Pentecost
Sunday of the Fulfillment
  Last Sunday after Pentecost

Minor Festivals

November

30 St. Andrew, Apostle*

December

21 St. Thomas, Apostle
26 St. Stephen, The First Martyr
27 St. John, Apostle and Evangelist
28 The Holy Innocents, Martyrs
31 New Year's Eve
    Eve of the Name of Jesus

January

 1 New Year's Day
    The Circumcision of Our Lord
18 The Confession of St. Peter
24 St. Timothy, Pastor and Confessor
25 The Conversion of St. Paul
26 St. Titus, Pastor and Confessor

February

 2 The Presentation of Our Lord
18 Martin Luther, Doctor and Confessor
24 St. Matthias, Apostle

March

25 The Annunciation of Our Lord

April

25 St. Mark, Evangelist

May

 1 St. Philip and St. James, Apostles
 7 C. F. W. Walther, Doctor
31 The Visitation

June

11 St. Barnabas, Apostle
24 The Nativity of St. John the Baptist
25 Presentation of the Augsburg Confession
29 St. Peter and St. Paul, Apostles

July

22 St. Mary Magdalene
26 St. James the Elder, Apostle

August

10 St. Laurence, Martyr
15 St. Mary, Mother of Our Lord
24 St. Bartholomew, Apostle

September

14 Holy Cross Day
21 St. Matthew, Apostle
     and Evangelist
29 St. Michael and All Angels

The Nativity
of John the Baptist

October

18 St. Luke, Evangelist
28 St. Simon and St. Jude, Apostles
31 Reformation Day

November

1 All Saints' Day
2 Commemoration of the Faithful Departed

*St. Andrew's Day determines the First Sunday in Advent and therefore
begins the enumeration of the minor festivals.

I Am Jesus' Little Lamb

I am Jesus' little lamb,
Ever glad at heart I am;
For my Shepherd gently guides me,
Knows my need and well provides me,
Loves me ev'ry day the same,
Even calls me by my name.

Day by day, at home, away,
Jesus is my staff and stay.
When I hunger, Jesus feeds me,
Into pleasant pastures leads me;
When I thirst, He bids me go
Where the quiet waters flow.

Who so happy as I am,
Even now the Shepherd's lamb?
And when my short life is ended,
By His angel host attended,
He shall fold me to His breast,
There within His arms to rest.

Henrietta L. von Hayn, 1724–82; tr. comp.

God's Own Child, I Gladly Say It

God's own child, I gladly say it:
I am baptized into Christ!
He, because I could not pay it,
Gave my full redemption price.
Do I need earth's treasures many?
I have one worth more than any
That brought me salvation free
Lasting to eternity!

Sin, disturb my soul no longer:
I am baptized into Christ!
I have comfort even stronger:
Jesus' cleansing sacrifice.
Should a guilty conscience seize me
Since my Baptism did release me
In a dear forgiving flood,
Sprinkling me with Jesus' blood?

Satan, hear this proclamation:
I am baptized into Christ!
Drop your ugly accusation,
I am not so soon enticed.
Now that to the font I've traveled,
All your might has come unraveled,
And, against your tyranny,
God, my Lord, unites with me!

Death, you cannot end my gladness:
I am baptized into Christ!
When I die, I leave all sadness
To inherit paradise!

Though I lie in dust and ashes
Faith's assurance brightly flashes:
Baptism has the strength divine
To make life immortal mine.

There is nothing worth comparing
To this lifelong comfort sure!
Open-eyed my grave is staring:
Even there I'll sleep secure.
Though my flesh awaits its raising,
Still my soul continues praising:
I am baptized into Christ;
I'm a child of paradise!

Erdmann Neumeister, 1671–1756; tr. Robert E. Voelker,
b. 1957

Lord, Help Us Ever to Retain

Lord, help us ever to retain
The Catechism's doctrine plain
As Luther taught the Word of truth
In simple style to tender youth.

Help us Your holy Law to learn,
To mourn our sin and from it turn
In faith to You and to Your Son
And Holy Spirit, Three in One.

Hear us, dear Father, when we pray
For needed help from day to day
That as Your children we may live,
Whom You baptized and so received.

Lord, when we fall or go astray,
Absolve and lift us up, we pray;
And through the Sacrament increase
Our faith till we depart in peace.

Ludwig Helmbold, 1532–98;
tr. Matthias Loy, 1828–1915, alt.

Martin Luther wrote
the Small Catechism in 1529.